See Something, Say Something
Who Do You Call

By William J. Riley

Published by Trikke.MI

WARNING
Procedures and Techniques Discussed Herein
Are Created and Apply Specifically to
The United States and Canada
Contact the Author for specific techniques for other countries

I0775959

Contents

Introduction 5

   Behaviors Especially Connected to Terrorism 5

Background 6

   Predators, Prey, Innocent Bystanders, Criminals and Terrorists 6

   Prey Types 8

   Predator Types 9

Behavior Profiling 10

   Behavior Profiling Inputs 11

Normal Behavior 11

   Abnormal Behavior 12

      At home or in private 12

      Outdoor 13

      Urban 13

      Commercial 13

   Summary of Abnormal Behavior 13

Detection by Old Criminalistics 14

Detection by New Criminalistics 15

Body Language 16

   Eyes 17

   Eye contact and Focus 17

   Smell 17

Body Language in General 18

Spatial Factors, also called Proxemics 19

What we do wrong 20

Characteristics of Criminal Behavior 21

   Limits of detection 22

Characteristics of Terrorist Behavior 22

   Social Media 22

   Regard for Life 22

   Motivation 22

   Religion 22

   Mental Illness 23

Prevention of Crime and Terrorism 23

Prediction 23

Timeline of Crime Including Terrorism 24

Behavior that should create suspicion 25

    Loitering 25

    Someone looks for a tail 25

    Someone follows you 25

    Standing Around 25

    Walking Aimlessly 25

    Driving Slowly 25

    Hyperawareness 25

    Eye contact svoidance 26

    Sitting for no reason 26

    Rider behavior 26

    Shopping behavior 26

    Watching the watchers 26

    Asking for change 26

    Looking for cameras 26

    Dress not suitable 26

    General 26

    Aggression 27

    Crime 27

Three Seconds to Safety 27

Detect, Protect and Report 27

Detecting terrorists in the early stages of an attack. 27

  Signs that could indicate preparation for terrorism 28

  Detect based on the environment 29

    In Home 29

    Outside 29

    Public or Commercial 29

    Outdoor Small Venue 29

    Outdoor Large Venue 29

    Indoor Large Venue 29

Protect 30

  At Home 30

Passive 30

Active 30

In public 31

Passive 31

Preventive 31

Suspicious behaviors 31

Report 32

Reporting Suspicions 32

WE NEED A NATIONAL SUSPICIOUS BEHAVIOR PHONE NUMBER!!! 32

Opinions...32

Guard Dogs/Cats...32

Violent Society 33

The myth of the good guy with a gun...33

The News Hole 33

Open Carry..33

Legal Training 33

Drug Crimes..34

Preventing Violence..34

Gangs 34

Car Jacking 35

Terrorists...35

Mental Illness...35

The Anti Movement..35

Crimes...35

Summary 36

Tools 36

Body Language Examples 37

Authors Expertise 38

References: 38

Suspicious Behavior Report 39

Introduction

The Author has been teaching Criminal Behavior Profiling to citizens for several years. The purpose of the seminars is to protect people from criminals by using their senses and the language of the body. Criminals look like everyone else, they dress like anyone and they can be of any ethnic group or nativity. The one key element to detect them is their behavior.

If you use any criteria except behavior you are at risk of being called a bigot and can be found to be in violation of the law. That is a high risk for law enforcement personnel since profiling (not the behavioral kind) has been deemed illegal by the highest courts.

Crime is a behavior that causes harm to a citizen and can range from intimidation to mass murder. Predators are the group of criminals who prey on people directly and with force. Terrorists prey on people for social, ethnic, racial, political religious and other reasons but not usually for money or valuables. There is also a type of criminal who commits crimes due to underlying mental illness and those crimes can range from petty theft to mass murder.

The Author wrote Predators 101 to support the seminars and to explain in some detail the exact methods of detecting criminal behavior and why the methods work. This book is an extension with some overlap. It is designed to address the problems of detecting and protecting against criminals and especially those who commit Terrorism. Terrorism is a superset of criminal behavior and requires attention to some additional behaviors.

My previous book, Predators 101 focused on detecting criminal behavior with the intent to encourage exiting the area for safety. The procedures in that book have proven successful. However we have come to believe that we need a different approach to radical terror threats.
In looking at that threat we believe that the perpetrator is different enough to require different analytical tools.

Behaviors Especially Connected to Terrorism

Criminals tend towards secrecy to avoid detection and prosecution. Terrorists often post warnings of future behavior and often brag about their actions after the fact. For this reason we need to examine both writing and speech behaviors. Also we need to consider social media as well as the normal media outlets.

The monitoring for what is normally called hate speech or hate literature is a job that requires every one's attention. The vast quantity and often limited distribution of that material such as closed mailing lists means that public scrutiny may be too little and too late.

This book will discuss legal elements but is not to be thought of as a LAW book but rather a general guide to areas that have legal risk. The Author is trained in the Law of Arrest and the Use of Lethal Force as well as Maritime Law and elements of the laws of war but is not prepared to offer legal advice.

We will focus on assigning names to actions and types of criminals to aid in understanding how things work. If you can name something you are on your way to understanding (and hopefully preventing) harmful behavior.

Background

Predators, Prey, Innocent Bystanders, Criminals and Terrorists

We can think of the civilian population (non military and non law enforcement) as divided into innocent bystanders, predators and prey. The predators that we consider terrorists are those who are not necessarily involved with their prey in a personal sense. The selected targets are usually strangers who can be symbolic or actual representatives of the terrorist target population.

We will keep the word predator for the balance of this book to mean both criminals and terrorists unless there is a need to identify their behavior separately.

Predators can be thought of as self-employed workers who train for their trade, have a place to "go to work" and have a set of tools. Some have formal training and some are self-taught.

The primary element that separates criminals from terrorists is the type of reward they seek. The criminal typically seeks some monetary goal or convertible asset. Terrorists often work towards an ideology which can be political, social, religious, ethnic or geographic.]

Criminals usually expect to survive the crime. Terrorists often focus on maximizing deaths or the destruction or both. They may or may not expect to survive

.

Criminals often target money or valuables but may seek other goals.

One key difference is the objective. Terrorists do not typically seek monetary reward as much as infamy. Their target is general destruction, mayhem and death. They may engage in fund raising for use in their efforts.

Criminals often have territories. Terrorists may have an area of operation that they focus on but I would not describe it is a territory.

Terrorists do not usually walk to work. They use transportation and often use the vehicle as a weapon.

Another difference is the disregard for their own survival. Most criminals want to reap the rewards for their endeavor. The obvious exception that comes to mind is "suicide by cop" but that is not the typical criminal and belongs in a third category.

The terrorist seems to work on a different time scale with months and years rather than weeks and days.

They both may do practice runs to enhance the success of their plan.

They both may operate as a loner or with a small group of associates. Most criminals do not identify with ideological elements such as religions, ethnic groups or political entities. Terrorists in large groups should be treated as war like combatants with detection and response based on military tactics.

Since the terrorists usually want higher body counts they tend more to public events where protection is more difficult.

Most criminals do not post details or video of their action. Police are lucky to catch surveillance data at all. Terrorists like to brag about their successes and often use social media to reach their audience. The criminal that does this is often young and thrill seeking and document their bad behavior in a show off sense. The chances are that they will be hurt by their action.

We cannot ignore the religious connection to many terror acts but we should recognize that religions seldom advocate death and destruction. That part seems to be pieced out of the cloth of the religion with some help from religious figures who feel persecuted or targeted by other elements of society.

In previous times the Public Libraries were research tools but it was not usually possible to tell what people were reading unless they checked the book out. Anything they read and returned to the shelf would have been difficult to track. If the person wanted to know how to make a bomb or work with poison they would have to seek out subject matter experts and that risked exposure.

Today the internet can tell you how to do almost anything and usually sell you the tools and products to complete the job. Yes, searching certain topics can raise flags but many products are not closely tracked. Chemistry can be a valuable skill area. The Dark Web is the other route that hinders tracking. It can be tracked but you have to be either unlucky or be a high value target.

Terrorists look like ordinary people. They dress like them, worship like them, go to school like them and work like them. The only way to recognize them is by their behavior. Before we get too far along that path I will point out that their behavior is like other predators (and that includes Police and other Security People).

Prey Types

Within the animal kingdom the predators often target the weak, lame, elderly, young and compromised prey. They do not seek a contest but food. Some prey animals engage in group behavior to protect the weak members.
Bees are known to have specialists such as the ventilating drones that keep the hive functioning. Ants also show specialization. Some animals post lookouts to warn of predators. Humans need to look at an alarm system to alert to predatory behavior from any source.

Alpha Males of most species are pretty safe but the range varies with different animals and humans seem to find new ways to ignore the potential and real threats to their safety. I have a section later listing what we do that increases our chances of becoming prey.

People can be their own watchman or they can create a protected area with a lookout to warn of predatory behavior. They are still responsible for taking cover or calling for help from the police or other security.

People can maximize their safety by keeping in groups, lowering their value as prey by their strength in numbers. It is especially important if anyone is physically handicapped or unhealthy. Predators like to take the easy target. It is also wise to avoid attracting attention by flashing money, jewelry or other valuables. If the person has high value targets such as expensive cars, the choice can be to engage protection or to increase alertness.

I would consider some animals to be built for others to prey on. They may have some defensive characteristics but usually offer little resistance once captured.

We also have animals who are aged, infirm, young or just careless.

Some animals seem built to be predators. They have lethal equipment such as claws or talons and fangs. They may have talents such as speed or strength but one characteristic seems typical. Predators tend to have forward facing eyes and binocular vision. Prey tend to have side facing eyes which are suited to keeping watch for predators.

Based on the physical characteristics, humans should find predation natural but controlled by socialization. They have become expert at using tools as weapons and they may use animals such as horses to give them speed.

When avoiding predatory behavior we should use all our tools and when handicapped we should join forces because two present a harder target than one.

Predator Types

Predators typically divide into two types, Ambush and Stalking. Ambush Predators lay in wait for prey, think Deer Blind. They can use bait like the deer hunter leaving carrots in front of their blind. They have surveilled the area and know the travel paths and escape routes, Stalking Predators follow their prey and pick the time and place to execute their attack.

We can learn to see basic predatory behavior by looking at the animal kingdom. A hawk circles in the sky watching for targets below. This is surveillance. Once prey is spotted the hawk dives down and snatches his meal. Once the dive begins it is usually too late for the victim. The answer is to interrupt the surveillance phase. We then try to get the prey out of harm's way.

The prey can post a lookout. When a bird flies into the area the lookout watches for predator behavior. An ordinary bird will fly from one place to another and a hawk will circle looking for a meal. The circling behavior of the hawk is the danger sign. When the lookout sees this predatory behavior they sound the alarm which sends everybody into hiding. Any that are slow to respond may become lunch.

Behavior Profiling

The basis of Behavior Profiling is Body Language which is how we communicate without words and Proxemics which is the way people use space. These two disciplines were first established by Dr. Edward T. Hall and defined in The Silent Language and The Hidden Dimension.

We will cover normal Body Language in this section but the Speech and Writing behaviors are separate for maximum clarity. Speech and Writing are more specific to terrorism detection and the detection of terrorist behavior can make use of the body language elements in this section.

Behavior does not exist in a vacuum. What is normal in one situation is abnormal in another so we need to consider the location of the behavior and the time. Time can refer to hours and minutes or seasons or special occasions. Locations vary from inside the home to wide open spaces with business, recreational and commercial locations in between.

When I speak of behavior I am talking mostly about gross behavior, we are not looking for small details. The person may be walking, talking, shopping, reading or some easily identified and namable activity.

When I began teaching Animation I was impressed by the fact that good animation followed real human behavior, especially body movement. Some teachers focused on getting lip, tongue and teeth accurately positioned for the words that were being used for the speaking track. I felt that timing was the important aspect since the earliest "animation" was the ventriliquist dummy. The dummies had only open mouth and close mouth but if they got the timing right it was believable.

Criminal behavior is not normal. We will look at normal behavior to establish a baseline for the purpose of identifying abnormal behavior in general. Once we are examining abnormal behavior we can look at what that means. Is it just odd behavior or does it mean probable criminal behavior? There are degrees of importance such as odd, dangerous, criminal and terroristic

Behavior Profiling Inputs

The inputs to Behavior Profiling are: Eyes-Vision, about 70 percent; Ears-Hearing, about 20 percent and Nose-Smell, about 10 percent. The exact percentage is unimportant except when trying to maintain protection. Many people wear glasses and those who don't often self-handicap by not keeping alert to the behavior of people in their vicinity.

Hearing loss is becoming increasingly common even in younger members of the population. This means that special attention should be paid to any noise that could signal danger. The specifics of alerting to behavior in the audio sphere have to do with noises made by objects. One recent problem that has turned up is with electric vehicles. There may be so little noise from the vehicle that blind people cannot detect them and that means more accidents.

Smell is the least useful tool because it tends to dissipate quickly and has to be strong to alert over distance. The obvious example for safety is the oderant added to natural gas to make leakage more detectable.
The fact that criminals often exhibit apocrine sweat is a good tool but you have to be close and the author's first principle is to avoid getting close if possible.

 Those who are handicapped in one or more of those spheres need to compensate as possible. The easiest compensation is to have a second set of eyes, ears and nose by having a companion. If the person has a support animal they should accept all alerts from their animal, especially due to the high sense of smell they usually have.

Normal Behavior

In the United States, most people are object oriented and task focused. They are clearly performing some task that we should be able to name or otherwise identify. They also demonstrate a lack of patience. They are typically in a hurry and, if driving, will pass anyone doing the speed limit.

Translation: We should not worry too much about people who pass us. It is the ones who follow behind, especially if they ignore opportunities to pass. The most common experience is that everybody is in a hurry and will pass you just to advance by one car.

It should be easy to identify the focus or task of anyone who spends time in our area. People who drift around or do not seem to be doing something identifiable are strongly suspect. They may be surveilling the area for future crime. They may be looking for immediate gain or they msy be waiting for a partner to arrive and better the odds of accomplishing their task.

I will stress that this suspicious behavior is not just indicative of criminal or terrorist behavior. It is entirely possible that you are looking at a Policeman, Loss Prevention Person, or other False Positive persona. It is still a good idea to get out of the area because the presence of such a person engaged in surveilling for crime could turn out to be a very danger signal.

Abnormal Behavior

We should feel comfortable amidst normal behavior even without instruction since it is "normal". We look at specifics which can change with the task or area. What is normal and abnormal can change with location.

Any behavior where dress in inappropriate for the task, the season or seems designed to hide the wearer can be suspect but certain items have become socially acceptable such as hooded sweatshirts.

Gangs have been known to wear clothing that will make identification more difficult or to confuse the observer/victim as to which one is to blame for harm.

At home or in private

That includes any area where family and friends are the normal group of people.

The most common Mass Murder in our society is a father who kills his children, his wife and then commits suicide so being at home is not necessarily safe.

Since this is private behavior we are not just looking for criminals or terrorists but we have to recognize that ordinary crime often involves people that we know or are related to.

The simplest way to approach this is to say that we should be cautious about any person's behavior that is escalating and points to harm to anyone including the person themselves. When investigating crimes law enforcement goes after the address book because the most common suspects are known to the victim.

Outdoor

Once we leave the home risk increases and in a suburban type area with neighbors the typical behavior will involve people going to or coming from work or play. If walking they will follow the shortest route from the activity to the home. It is not out of the ordinary to stop briefly and chat with neighbors. If driving they will typically enter the car, start it and drive away. When returning they will park close to home, exit and enter the house or apartment.

Any lack of attention to the apparent task is suspect. For example, walking a dog requires some attention to and response to the dog's actions.

Urban

Parking space in urban areas is usually scarce so walking from a bus stop is much more common than in suburban areas. Whether walking or driving the behavior is usually straight line when leaving or returning. The other common behavior is walking a pet. This seldom results in predictable behavior but is seldom suspect.

Commercial

Shoppers will usually try for the closest place to the store or the entrance. Whether singly or in small groups, the shoppers will be swift and direct in their path.

Summary of Abnormal Behavior

Abnormal behavior is always suspicious. It needs to be reported and that requires that you describe the behavior clearly and simply. The way to detect abnormal behavior is to look at the body language.

You should be able to name the behavior of anyone in your environment. What they are doing is not as important as the fact you can name it. Loitering is the classic case of suspicious behavior. The criminal looks for prey and valuables and waits for opportunity. That involves looking busy because they do not want people watching them. They prefer not being identifiable and will often try to blend into the environment.

Detection by Old Criminalistics

The science of crime prevention began when police were given a territory to patrol. They became familiar with the residents and knew who was visiting. They knew the behavior in most cases. Unusual behavior drew attention and potential misbehavior was often handled before it deteriorated to the level of crime.

The major analytic tool was Pin Mapping. Pins of different colors were used on a map of the area. By observation, patterns and hot spots were perceived and often proved useful in solving crimes.

Crimes which occurred were handled by Detectives and other specialists evolved such as Evidence Technicians. Some forces were called out as needed for major events, parades and crowds.

Detection of predators is everyone one's responsibility. Every person has to be vigilant. A group of people may have someone assigned as the primary watchman but all should keep an eye out for predatory behavior.

My book, Predators 101, teaches 3 Seconds to Safety. If someone in your environment has attracted your attention, ask - What are they doing? If you cannot answer that in simple terms within 3 seconds it may be a predator and you need to get out of harms way,

Police and Security personnel exhibit the same behavior... They are Predators but their prey is the criminals and terrorists in our midst. This is called a false positive but speaking as a retired Deputy Sheriff, if I am in Predatory mode you should get out of the area because it is likely going to be very HOT! Perhaps including weapon use.

Detection by New Criminalistics

Science has produced tools to assist in predicting crime and criminal behavior. The scientific method applied to law enforcement has resulted in mapping and statistical analysis tools.

Crime Mapping grew from the Pin Maps of the early days. The most serious defect of the pin mapping system was the lack of time information. The "where" could be obvious but the fact that crime occurs in time as well as space was not made visible.

Environmental Science Research Institute (ESRI) was produces software that is used by cities to handle tax and property data. Some enterprising Criminologists discovered it and the company began developing what is now called Crime Mapping. This tool allows users to incorporate time into the equation. In the best cases, where two or more crimes can be associated with the same perpetrator, the software has been useful in locating the perpetrator(s).

Handwriting analysis
The Author uses Handwriting Analysis as a general tool in the Criminal Behavior Profiling procedure. In seminars the Author discusses the workings that are appropriate to the profiling task. Specific questions should be directed to the Author by email.

Voice analysis
Voices are unique and verbal data can provide useful information. The tone and stress of speech change with the changes in facial features such as smiling and also change when the subject is lying. There are instruments available to determine scientifically what is happening. The Author uses voice recognition as a major tool. Specific questions should be directed to the Author by email.

Path to Crime
Criminals typically have a method that they become comfortable with and that method often becomes the clue to catching them. If a criminal commits only a single crime it is very difficult to catch them. On the second or further crimes they begin the end game.

Body Language

Body Language is something that we learn without paying attention to it. We compare how we are treated by the people close to us such as our parents. The result of this process is often called intuition or "a gut feeling".

You started learning body language when you were born and by the time you were six months old you could easily detect the difference between the behavior of "good" people and "bad" people. You would not have been able to tell how you did it but you would react to others. The good behavior should have been that of your parents, siblings and family friends.

Simply put, people who did not meet the standards of "good" would be reacted to in a negative manner. In Predators 101 I discuss the sense of smell with particular regard to bad behavior.

Body Language can be looked at on a micro level where eye blink and muscle tone are significant and that can be significant to the professional analyst. We do not see that level of attention as productive. We will be looking at gross behavior and which behaviors merit concern. Be aware that we do not advise interaction with the criminal, only avoidance. The formula is Detect, Protect and Report. This has been called "Be Your Own Bodyguard" and that is exactly what a bodyguard would do, they would get you out of harm's way.

Body Language that we consider important is stance, gait, direction of movement and direction of gaze. We also look at the sum of movements and the environment in which the behavior occurs. We will discuss Normal Behavior and Abnormal Behavior for specific circumstances. There will be guidance on how to report the abnormal behavior to ensure prompt and proper attention is given by law enforcement.

Typically, humans read body language by the age of six months and usually express their reading by the use of words like "intuition", a "hunch" or it just feels right.

Minor components are the facial muscles and positioning of hands and feet. My focus on this area is involved in voice analysis. You can tell if someone is smiling without seeing them because the tone of voice is changed by those facial muscles.

Eyes

Eyes and what they look at form the most basic inputs. We look at things we like or want. We can tell what others are looking at by analyzing the focal point of their pupils. It is automatic in adults. In sports we are told to "keep our eyes on the ball". The result is that we project the arc and the time of travel to put our glove or our bat in position to intercept the ball.

The hallway dance is another example of this eye communication. When two people are about to pass each other in the hallway they look to the left or right to let the other person know where they will shift to pass. When one of them lies with their eyes they both wind up on the same side.

Eye contact and Focus

Predators look at prey

Predators look at objects that they want

Decoy objects
The Author wears a handcuff case watching for a recognition response which would come from someone in law enforcement or someone who has been handcuffed.

Smell

We have two sweat systems, ecrine and apocrine. Ecrine sweat does not decompose so it does not smell. Apocrine sweat starts decomposing as soon as it reaches the surface of the skin. That produces the typical "sweaty" aroma.

Ecrine sweat is released to cool the body. Apocrine sweat is release by fear, hate and other strong emotions.

Criminals of all sorts are typically in fear of being detected so they will be likely to have apocrine sweat. The other triggers are strong emotions such as anger. Think of the phrase "I smell a rat!"

Body Language in General

Keep your eye on the ball is the familiar refrain for golf, baseball, tennis and it is based on calculating the future position if the ball is in motion and projecting an intersection in time and space or for golf, putting the club into contact with the ball to cause motion.

Zen Archers can hit a bird in flight with a bow and arrow. Good but when you find they are blind we have to figure out how it is done. My conclusion is that they are echo locating the bird and projecting it's position to intersect with the arrow.

Zen Aim is my term for the Sheriff Department training on the Gun Range. Lay the forefinger alongside the barrel. You have been pointing at things all your life and you simply have to have faith in the process.

Evil Eye is the expression for the ability of the eye to cause behavior in the world. I will simply say that we can tell if someone is looking at us at some distance and we have learned that when someone is looking it may be with the intent to take the item they are looking at.

Steering a bicycle
You do not turn the handle bar of your bicycle to make a turn. You simply look where you want to go and your body expresses that wish by creating the necessary movement.

You can tell if someone is looking at you over a distance. You detect the object they are looking at by watching the pupils of their eyes. You can tell where their focus is.

Spatial Factors, also called Proxemics

One of the earliest use of Proxemics was the discovery in warfare that the force occupying the higher ground had control of the territory. Height in general confers power.

Another factor is how close people are to each other. Personal space is the area within arms reach for most western groups. Some others will pull strangers close but for most this is the realm for family and very close friends.

Social space is the near area beyond handshake distance. This is where business takes place and many public interactions.

Public space is the area where we may know who the people are but it can include strangers.

Height factors. Research has concluded that taller people are generally more successful and platforms can elevate people to some degree to either increase their power or to recognize the power that they exert.

Threat postures and movements. Raising the hand or arm can be a threat but palm turned toward the observer is showing the lack of a weapon so becomes neutral. Pulling the arm back is often a precursor to striking a boxing type blow.

What we do wrong

Predictability
Stalking Predators track down their victim so following behavior is particularly bad but the Ambush Predator counts on you being habitual. In either case there is no penalty for being unpredictable.

Not locking things
If people simply locked their doors, lockers and cars the crime rate would probably drop by fifty percent.

No escape plan
Most people realize the need for fire drills and practice for other emergencies. We should all be aware of our surroundings and know what to do if we have to get to safety. Locate the exits and have a plan to meet in a safe location.

Stopping a car without locking the door.
Many cars lock the doors as soon as the engine starts running. Predators often try to open car doors and succeed because they were unlocked.

People walk away from their car without checking the door locks.
I know that the automatic locks operate in most cases. Now, if electronics never failed I could understand not checking but I know better. One time out of five, the lock button on my remote locks the driver door but not the sliding door. It is an old car but if an old one can fail, a brand new one can fail. Why else would we have recalls for failed parts.

Getting in car without checking back seat area
Cars can be opened by crooks with tools and hiding on the floor or back seat area is one of the ways people get robbed.

Limiting our senses
I have seen a walker with ear buds on reading a book. Yes, it was daylight, it was a nice neighborhood and yes, there were other people around (mostly me). Many a robbery has occurred in such nice conditions. Criminals like to work in nice weather too.

If you cannot jog or walk without listening to music or other things that interfere with hearing at least have someone with you to monitor the area for predators.

People often create what we call an attractive nuisance. That is something that is attractive to trespassers, thieves or other anti-social persons. This could be flashing money, wearing Designer clothes or expensive jewelry in the wrong places, leaving locks unlocked or otherwise creating a possibility of reward for a low risk. If people simply locked the locks on their doors, lockers, cars etc. we would probably reduce the crime rate by fifty percent. When I look at crime reports for the average urban area they are filled with thefts from unlocked cars, houses, lockers and garages.

People in the United States have some common traits that abet criminal behavior and some that help identify the criminals. The most common bad thing that we do is to be predictable. We like to have schedules and stick to them. Criminals become expert at identifying patterns of behavior for the same reason that hunters observe the behavior of their prey. It makes their job easier if they can predict when and where you will appear. Of course there are things that need to be predictable such as getting to work on time but we can change our route from time to time. We definitely should not get gas at the same station at the same time. A lot of car-jackings have taken place at gas stations and Mall parking lots. It is difficult to hijack a moving car but once it stops make sure all doors are locked and avoid stopping where there is no one around.

Characteristics of Criminal Behavior

Territory
Criminals usually have a territory that they are comfortable with. They know the escape routes, the normal targets and their behavior. Terrorists are different in that they have a new area for each action unless they become embedded in which case they can be treated as combatants and warfare techniques become appropriate.

So, from a territorial standpoint they need to surveil the area for their crime anew. We can evaluate the targets that are available and when they match the objectives of the terror based group we raise the threat level and prevention becomes the best approach.

Target Selection and Risk Reward Analysis
Every target presents with a risk and a reward. The criminal has to find that the expected reward is worth the expected risk. We have three paths that we can follow. We can raise the risk or we can reduce the reward value. We can do both.

High Value, Low Value
When we reduce the apparent value of a target we reduce the chance that a predator will be attracted. Flashing jewelry, money or convertible goods is a sure method of attracting predatory behavior. People with no perceived value have to worry about predators who are out to hurt people.

Limits of detection
Criminals that commit a single crime often are undetected. It is a second crime which usually begins the detection and analysis process.

Characteristics of Terrorist Behavior
How does Crime raise to the level of terrorism? Research indicates that violent criminals are often known to their victims. When crimes are committed by strangers and instigated by targeting religion, race, ethnicity, geographic location, political affiliation or some other characteristic (not money or convertible asset) it is safe to call it terrorism.

Social Media
How terrorists differ from common criminals. A common characteristic of terrorist crimes is the use of social media to record, forecast or otherwise make public the responsible group or person.

Regard for Life
Disregard for personal safety or life of the person responsible. Suicide bombers for example. The goal in most terrorist acts is to maximize the loss of life.

Motivation
The motive is often political or religious in nature rather than money or money substitutes. Fund raising for terrorism is often pursued outside of the criminal arena. Fame or notoriety is another common feature.

Religion
Criminals do not normally seek a particular religion or philosophy for their crimes. Terrorists often are guided by a religious belief. The Jonestown Massacre terror crime was built on a religion based group. The members were convinced by the leader to commit suicide by drinking poison. The terror in this case was limited to the group.

Mental Illness

Mental illness of some type, can be a direct cause or trigger for criminal behavior at any level.

Prevention of Crime and Terrorism

Whether crime or terrorism, prevention is the first goal. It is not romantic or exciting. A negative outcome is difficult or impossible to prove but is the objective.

Prevention can be approached by hardening the target. This requires identification of a target and then assembling a protective perimeter and examining entering threats. Someone should be watching the parking areas because criminals and terrorists often drive to the crime scene and, when carrying long guns, are easy to spot.

If we cannot identify a target or harden the perimeter then we have to intercept all threats that enter the area of concern. The criminal only has to succeed once.

If prevention is not achieved then we want to mitigate damage. Rapid response by law enforcement, emergency services and triage personnel is achieved through practice runs.

Prediction

Abnormal behavior is a strong predictor of crime at all levels including terrorism. Threats should never be ignored but unless the threat includes the real possibility of harm it would not normally call for police involvement.

Threat behavior which includes a strong potential for harm can be a crime in itself. The charge would be Assault.

If the threat is stronger than is reasonable and carries on over time it should be reported as suspicious behavior. Everyone can become upset and show strong emotions or responses but it should dissipate in a short time. Anyone expressing anger over an extended period of time and especially if they threaten violence should be reported.

Knowledge of past criminal behavior should raise the alert level to a high degree.

Everyone deserves the benefit of doubt but no one should endure high risk behavior lightly.

Probably the biggest difference between crime and terrorism is that crime prediction is mostly based on group behavior. We have high crime areas and low crime areas. They are tracked by law enforcement. They may be connected to the presence of a high value targets such as jewelry or some other high value target. Terrorists are the target of law enforcement and our Intelligence community using sophisticated surveillance tools and mechanisms.

Timeline of Crime Including Terrorism

Typical stages of crime

Planning stage consists of looking for likely targets and evaluating their danger level. If the target is difficult or protected most predators will seek out an easier prey.

If we can interrupt the planning stage of crime we enhance our safety at the least cost and best chance of success.

Prepare toolbox
Predators often use tools in crimes. They may also wear a disguise to prevent or delay identification.

Act
Once a predator is at work the danger level is maximum and an attack is more difficult to stop than in the planning stage.

Escape
In most cases the criminal is bent on escape as soon as possible.
Terrorists may not plan to escape.

Exploit.
When the criminal feels safe they may exploit their gains. Terrorists may brag about their success

Behavior that should create suspicion

Loitering

Loitering in many areas can be a crime and is still the favorite tool of criminals. They get to know the target area and check for escape routes.

Someone looks for a tail

If someone is constantly checking behind them as they travel they could be checking to see if they are being followed. It is very suspicious if they cross and re-cross the street.

Someone follows you

You need to be very suspicious if someone is following you. You need to verify their behavior by introducing unneeded changes in you path to see if they continue to follow. If this happens you need to get help as quickly as possible. The only reasonable explanation would be if you were famous.

Standing around

Americans are not usually just standing around. They would be doing something and often more than one thing.

Walking aimlessly

Walking without purpose. Walking aimlessly is extremely rare. Pacing back and forth is an exception if the environment is suitable such as a hospital.

Driving slowly

You can usually ignore anyone driving slightly above the speed limit. It is almost a requirement for driving. Those who drive below the speed limit, unless obviously looking for an address, turning point or such are suspicious. If a police car is in the area and the slow driver avoids eye contact it is almost certain that the driver is doing something wrong.

Hyperawareness

Hyperawareness is almost a guarantee of problems because criminals are very sensitive to being caught or trapped. They are constantly checking for cameras and escape routes.

Eye contact avoidance

Seeing eye to eye is a trait for agreement between people. Inability to look someone in the eye is suspect unless you know that the person is bashful in the extreme or otherwise unsocial.

Sitting for no reason

Americans can seldom sit without multitasking.

Rider behavior

Public transportation passengers should be wary of any body contact which could be pickpocket behavior. One suspicious place is at the exit, especially if there are other seats available. They may be planning a grab and exit at a stop. Most people will spread out among the empty seats.

Shopping behavior

People who are shopping will be consistent in looking at the merchandise and not at the environment.

Watching the watchers

At performances, most people will be looking at the show perhaps with a casual check of where their children or friends are. People who are focused on the crowd are very suspicious

Asking for change

This is a common ploy to see what is in the cash register. Customers actually needing change are most likely going to buy some cheap item just to be neighborly but most places just do not need change.

Looking for cameras

Only a security person would normally look at and for cameras. Most people would never bother.

Dress not suitable

One of the most important danger signals is dress that is not appropriate for the task, the weather or the situation.

General

Inappropriate behavior of any kind - trying to open a car door with a housekey

Aggression

Aggressive behavior such as the knockout game

Crime

Any crime is automatically suspicious behavior. One of the newer crimes is Apple picking - the term for grabbing a cell phone from someone.

Three Seconds to Safety

Look around. If someone is near you ask the simple question: What are they doing. You should be able to state in simple words, they are reading, shopping, walking or some task. If you cannot do that they are to be suspect and you should begin with the **Detect, Protect, Report** protocols. They are legitimate suspects for criminal behavior ranging from petty theft to terrorism. Caution, you should not take corrective action, you should report your suspicion. The only time for direct response is if they are in the process of committing a crime. In that case you seek shelter and call 911.

Detect, Protect and Report

Detecting terrorists in the early stages of an attack.

The FBI and all associated agencies have been sensitive to Social Media postings as a first tool for finding the seeds of terrorism. This seems to be related to the need for publicity for terror. Most criminals do not wish to be caught so they keep a lid on publicity.

Terrorists often want publicity for their actions. They may signal their intent by postings and they may brag about what happened. Such postings should be reported when spotted. If they turn out to be harmless then no damage but if they result in higher security which in turn prevents a crime then all the better.

The problem is quantity. There is an immense amount of data and reading by law enforcement is not a priority. Everyone needs to participate in locating the first signs of that behavior. Restraint in action while investigating is the rule and dead ends are acceptable. Software can scan for certain key words but the terrorists seem to move into new areas where alerts are not going to come from automated tools. They learn from their failures and spend a lot of effort on research and development.

Signs that could indicate preparation for terrorism
Surveillance - more than just "looking around"
Using binoculars for looking when not appropriate
In partial uniform or mixed, also dressed inappropriately for the time, season, temperature etc.
Gathering information that isn't for historic or traditional purposes or just asking strange questions.
Testing security in any way including trespassing
Photography other than for obvious and recognizable purposes
Unusual purchases or packages
Ignoring the attraction at any event. This is also called "watching the watchers". It is normal to routinely check on your kids or relatives at these events but when the main attraction is ignored then you have to ask "what are they here for?" The most common answer is CRIME!

Perhaps the most difficult task is to determine when someone is assembling equipment to use in a terror attack.

Take guns, someone may have 1,000 guns but if they are unique and historic it might be a museum in waiting. Another may have five guns but if they are all assault rifles I would suspect that something is wrong. Two, even three could be ordinary but the fourth and fifth seems to be excessive for target, hunting or protection. If they have high capacity magazines it increases my suspicions.

In the ammunition area, hunting ammunition quantities over a hundred seems excessive. Target rounds likewise since you probably do not want to use old ammo. Armor piercing rounds in any quantity should sound an alarm.

Another factor is when purchased. Ammo might be bought monthly if the shooter goes to the range on a regular basis. Large purchase amounts over a short period should raise questions.

When your integrated senses tell you that something is wrong...report your suspicions!

Detect based on the environment

In Home

If you are in your home you have a very low risk of being a terrorist target. You do however have to consider the potential for domestic violence. The first place we look for clues in these situations whether at work or in the home is the address book of the victim. In most cases the assailant is someone they know.

Outside

When we expand to the neighborhood we begin our examination for criminal behavior from people that we would consider strangers. Neighborhoods can be territories for ordinary criminals or if the neighborhood has a concentration of ethnic, political or religious groups, we should consider the potential for terror activity.

Public or Commercial

Commerce and industry are often the focus for ordinary criminals but because they often involve larger groups of people, especially if they have commonalities of one sort or another we should look for terrorist behavior with greater attention to gatherings.

Outdoor Small Venue

Small concentrations of people in a general outdoor setting such as a park or recreational facility begin to be serious targets for some terrorists, especially if the area has ethnic or religious focus.

Outdoor Large Venue

Large outdoor functions are a primary target for terrorist type activity

Indoor Large Venue

Stadiums, Arenas and such are definite targets for terror activity, especially since they often have limited ability to escape from.

Methods of detecting both criminal and terrorist activity are similar since the most common precursor to either activity is surveillance.

Criminals and terrorists need to know the area where they will operate and they have to prepare for arrival, action and departure. They often will make trial runs to check out their plans. This is the best time to interrupt their plans. If you wait until the plan is executed it will usually be too late to stop or even decrease the mayhem.

Surveillance behavior almost always involves loitering type behavior. As described in Predators 101, the persons behavior will be difficult to describe since there will be no goal except knowledge. They will not seem to be doing anything. This behavior will typically be associated with a future event of some kind that will bring target groups into focus.

If you have a future event that could be the target of a terrorist group you will need to control access to targets very closely and keep your senses on high alert for any unusual behavior.

Protect

At Home
Inside your home should not be dangerous but considering that criminals are often known to the victim you will want to pay attention to behavior changes in your friends, neighbors and relatives.

In my seminars the protection part is now called "Be Your Own Bodyguard". If you think about it, if you are rich and have a bodyguard their job is to get you away from trouble. Well, just take yourself out of the trouble area.

Passive
The phrase "attractive nuisance" refers to objects or conditions that encourage targeting. Reduce target value by hiding or removing attractors.

Active

This is limited advice because the author is not a fan of armed intervention by non-law enforcement people. The best action is to get to safety by the quickest way possible and immediately call 911 to get help. You have a plan in case fire breaks out, you should have one in case someone breaks in.

In public

Passive

The phrase "attractive nuisance" refers to objects or conditions that encourage targeting. Decrease target value by hiding or removing attractors.

Another method of protection is to find hot spots using services such as "crimemapping.com" to assist you in avoiding threat areas or to alert you to the need for more vigilance.

You Don't Have to Outrun the Bear

There is not only safety in numbers but keep in mind that you have to protect stragglers when leaving a danger area. Criminals will go for the weakest members of the prey group. Terrorists are going for maximum damage and may have little or no concern from their own fate

Preventive

 Using tools like crimemapping.com you can avoid Danger areas, Danger times and Hot spots in general. Your local Police should be able to advise you of areas to avoid.

Broken Window theory says that well maintained areas are safer than areas that have been left to decay. There is certainly some evidence that criminals prefer areas that receive less attention because they seek privacy for their behavior and the concept is that clean areas are watched more closely

Attractive nuisance it term for any building, area or activity (sports equipment) that brings people together with little or no supervision.

Suspicious behaviors

Why do Police look for casual disobedience of "minor laws"?
First, big criminals often commit small crimes. Approximately one third of traffic stops will find people with open warrants for serious crimes.
In their haste, many people coast through stop signs, exceed the speed limit and pass on the right side. The suspicious behavior is often exaggerated compliance.

Avoiding eye contact, especially with Police is a very suspicious behavior. The phrase used by Law Enforcement is the "you can't see me if I don't see you."

Another specific behavior is the manner of dress. If someone is jogging they are likely to be in exercise gear. A suit would be inappropriate and would be suspicious. Running in street shoes would be suspect.

Uniforms tend to identify safe individuals but predators can adopt them as protective coloration. They often do not get it right. They may mix the parts wrong or have the wrong decoration or badge or ID. The average person may not be able to detect the fakery but behavior will still be a tool to alert.

Report

Reporting Suspicions

The single biggest problem that we face is the lack of a simple reporting system. The phrase that titles this book, See Something, Say Something sounds good but the reality is that the average person has little or no training in who to notify if they have suspicions. There are often eight to ten phone numbers that can be used to notify law enforcement about suspicious behavior. The citizen is usually aware that calling 911 is for **Crimes in Progress Only** but there is no other one stop method.

WE NEED A NATIONAL SUSPICIOUS BEHAVIOR PHONE NUMBER!!!

I HAVE INCLUDED A SUGGESTED REPORT FORM ON THE LAST PAGE

Opinions

Guard Dogs/Cats

Dogs and cats can do an excellent job of alerting you to strangers. I believe it is misuse of their talent to expect them to guard your belongings from theft. They are easily defeated by a determined criminal and they would probably not hesitate to kill them in the process. They should not be put in harm's way by civilians. Military and K-Nine Corps are trained and under the control of a trained Soldier or Police Officer

Violent Society

One characteristic of American society is the number of handguns per capita. Another is the fascination with the old west where disputes were often resolved with weapons with or without the involvement of the criminal justice system.

The myth of the good guy with a gun

We have supplied the world with a romanticized picture of the wild west. Our heros of that era often had a cloudy past and a fast draw was the key to success. We are still hostage to the idea that guns are tools in the battle between good and evil. In the movies the good guys always win and the bad guys go to jail or the grave.

The News Hole

There is a system for media reporting on news. The space for presenting stories is limited and the market for particular types of stories changes over time and in different places. The Editor looks for items that will draw readership and thereby increase profits. With rare exceptions, news is meant to be profitable.

What winds up getting published is what will fit into the "news hole. It is the space left over after required elements. Since the front page is premium territory the Publisher divides that space into columns and fits as many stories as he can into that prime space.

Open Carry

Open carry by someone not in uniform and on duty is tactical suicide. You have given up the element of surprise.

Legal Training

Law enforcement personnel are trained in the legal use of force and especially lethal force. You cannot legally use lethal force against a property crime, you also cannot legally use more force than is necessary to stop the crime. Police are often sued and sometimes lose.

I have heard some say that many people have more range time than active duty Law Enforcement personnel. That may be true but time on the range is not a factor. The simple way to look at this concept is that if you have a leak you may be able to stop it yourself but if it is serious you may need a plumber. Law Enforcement Officers are professionals. Even if the citizen is equally trained they will have to get their own lawyer if the actions become a court case.

In the movies you could tell the good guys from the bad ones by the color of their hats. In war you can tell the bad guys by their uniform.
On the street, non uniformed armed personnel can be undercover police or they can be criminals. Police take care of their undercover brothers/sisters and have established protocols to protect them. Any non recognized armed individual is at least for a time a potential target and contributes to the fog of combat.
There is the problem of liability for harm done to someone in the encounter. It would not be the first time the suspect in a crime filed suit for injury.

Drug Crimes

We have a long history of using legal prohibition to suppress alcoholism and other self- harming behaviors. If people want to use drugs, alcohol or such they are hard to stop. Making drug abuse a crime introduces a profit motive and we make millionaires out of petty criminals. If the actions are de-criminalized then the profit motive is removed and the dealers will have to go to work at McDonalds,

Preventing Violence

We have problems in preventing violence regardless of the level but looking at the different kinds of violence should be a step in the right direction. To name the beast is to begin taming it.

The simplest form of violence is that which is self inflicted.

The next stage is one on one violence and the sub levels depend on the form and amount of the reward. Either the target or the assailant can be a company or group.

Gangs

Gangs typically depend on intimidation to prevent or deter detection. If the gang can be sure of prosecution and justice for their deeds they will usually find a better way of life. Only as long as they can reliably escape punishment will they keep to the mischief.

Car Jacking

It is very difficult and dangerous to stop a moving vehicle. This means that the best protection against car jacking is to keep the vehicle in motion. If you have any reason to suspect this crime do not stop until you are in protected areas such as Police Departments. Even marked vehicles can be used by criminals. If you suspect anything you should contact the Police by cell phone to explain what is happening and let them know that you are not fleeing a legitimate stop, only ensuring that you are not in danger. You should never be stopped by an unmarked vehicle but markings alone are not enough to ensure lack of criminal behavior.

Terrorists

When you hear a story about terrorism it is easy to become fearful. It is far more useful to become alert. Terrorism is crime on a big scale and most crimes are committed by someone you know or are related to unless you have been signaling that you are a high value target with compromised protection.

Mental Illness

This country has a problem knowing how to handle Mental Illness. In bygone times we had confined patients to Mental Hospitals and controlled their behavior through medication and/or forceful restraint. When civil rights concerns made that difficult or impossible we have problems if people resist treatment or support.

The Anti Movement

There are groups of people who have adopted a policy that only Sheriffs have legitimate authority to perform police functions. They base this on the fact that Sheriffs are elected and so derive their authority from the consent of the governed. They physically resist efforts by non Sheriff law enforcement at all levels including the use of deadly force.

Crimes

There are levels of crime:

Civil Infractions are violation of rules that typically require payment of a fine but not jail.

Misdemeanors are violations that can result in jail time and/or fines.
Felonies are serious violations that can extend to life imprisonment or the death penalty.

-The Boston Marathon
Two brothers used bombs designed to maximize casualties and targeted a random group of innocents.

Pulse Nightclub, The Florida Massacre, June, 2016 49 killed
The gunman drove to the bar and exited that vehicle with a long gun. Undetected until he opened fire points out that someone should have been watching the parking area. This would have been some help but probably not enough.

Summary

Tools

Whistle should be the Acme Thunderer. The Acme was the original Police whistle and will make your ears ring. Cheaper ones do not work. Having it on a chain or lanyard makes it available quickly.

Flashlight with a lanyard if possible. In day time it can be a baton, at night it can temporarily blind a criminal. Rechargeable batteries can save money over the long run.

Pepper Spray. You can save money by just using real pepper. Local regulations may apply but Mace is generally illegal since it can damage the cornea.

Cane might be an assist in walking but is a big stick and can deter some including animals that have an attack attitude.

Dummy Wallet. NOTE: Get a used one from the Thrift store, it looks more credible and is a good storehouse for all those fake credit cards you get in the mail. Throw a few real dollars in to complete the illusion.

Dummy Keys or real keys. If you choose to have only your real keys and the criminal wants them, you may want to throw them as far as possible. If you want to keep decoy keys then just give them up.

Locks are useless unless they are used to lock something.

Best way to park Think about fast exit. Back in if allowed then you can speed away. Do not allow yourself to be blocked in. Try to have light on all sides. Darkness is a criminals best friend. When approaching your car after it has been parked, check back seat before entering.

Best lockers to use. Go for the ones most visible to passersby. The end one on the aisle.

Bolt Cutters vs cables
Bolt cutters are made to break solid steel type locks. They are of little use on wire rope. They are difficult to conceal. Bicycles are safer with the wire cables.

Body Language Examples

Case Study 1 Boat Stop
Sheriff attempted a boat stop. Boat operator fled and report was made to Dispatch. Dispatch was visually monitoring traffic in the channel. Boat was noted entering the inbound channel from the direction of the attempted stop. Description of the boat did not match report but the boat crossed the channel and proceeded towards port but beyond a breakwater. That is not normal behavior. It would have been quicker and shorter to proceed in the channel. The boat entered the channel at a gap which allowed vessels access to the channel without going all the way to the entrance. The suspicious behavior caused Dispatch to use binoculars to see the operator. The operator did not match the description but he looked behind himself to see if he was being followed. That was the action of a guilty party and when Dispatch sent a chase boat they caught the operator and a citation was issued.

Case Study 2 Olongopo Market
The author was in a public market near Subic Bay. This was during the period that Headhunters would come down from their mountain hide outs and create mayhem which included killing the Police Chief on the steps of city hall.
He saw a man dressed in a trench coat loitering under a lamppost and a Thompson sub-machine was observed under the coat. Suspicious behaviors: Temperature was in the 90's, coat was suspicious. Loitering was suspicious. The situation was resolved when it was discovered that the man was an "undercover" Policeman. The Police Car (a jeep with a .50 caliber machinegun mounted) stopped to chat with the man.

Case Study 3 Car stop
While driving in an alley to enter a Freeway service drive the author suddenly stopped his vehicle. There was no visible reason to stop. In a moment, a State Police vehicle backed on the service drive at a high rate of speed. The author would have been hit if he had not stopped. The analysis was that the author heard a vehicle accelerating rapidly from right to left when any acceleration should have been from left to right. This contradiction was passed to the brain which halted all movement. Typically halting is the safest thing to do in most unknown situations.

Authors Expertise

BA Sociology, Oakland University, 1973
Minor in Art History
Teaching Certificate, Secondary Education, All Subjects
Specialist in Electronic Warfare, U.S. Navy, 1967
Deputy Sheriff, Macomb County Sheriff Department, Marine Division, Retired
Writer, Editor and Publisher
College Teacher, 3D Modeling, Animation
Consultant, Manufacturing, Electric Vehicles
Factory Representative, Electric Police Vehicles

References:

Brent Smith; Ph.D, Director of Terrorism Research Center, (TRC) in Fulbright College, University of Arkansas

Carl Chinn, Church Security Consultant, Colorado Springs, Colorado

Chris Shields, Ph.D, Asst. Prof and American Terrorism Study Project Manager

Dallas Drake, Senior Researcher, Center for Homicide Research

Danial Burke; CNN Religion Editor

Fred Burton; stratfor.com Chief Security Officer
Counterterrorism Intelligence Report in Police one.com News
Watching for watchers: The warning signs of terrorist behavior

Suspicious Behavior Report

If a crime is in progress call 911, for suspicious behavior call the local Police
Dispatch at____
They will likely ask for the following data:

Location____

Your name, address and phone number or other contact information

Description of the suspect____

Vehicle____

Behavior____

Other phone numbers

City Hall____

Sheriff Dispatch____

State Police Dispatch______________________________________

Game Warden____

FBI____

Department of Homeland Security_______________________________

Alcohol, Tobacco and Firearms______________________________

United States Coast Guard__________________________________